The Bird of Endless Time

The Bird of Endless Time

POEMS BY JAMES LAUGHLIN

COPPER CANYON PRESS : PORT TOWNSEND

SOME OF THESE POEMS FIRST APPEARED IN *The American Voice, Antaeus, Chelsea, Conjunctions, Exquisite Corpse, Interim, Kentucky Poetry Review, New American Writing, New York Quarterly, Paris Review, Poetry, The Quarterly, Scripsi, Sud, Third Rail, West Coast Review, The Yale Review,*
AND IN THE BOOK *Kollemata* (STINEHOUR PRESS)

ISBN 1-55659-020-2 (CLOTH)
ISBN 1-55659-021-0 (PAPER)

LIBRARY OF CONGRESS CARD NUMBER 88-63226
THE PUBLICATION OF THIS BOOK WAS SUPPORTED BY A GRANT FROM THE NATIONAL ENDOWMENT FOR THE ARTS. COPPER CANYON PRESS IS IN RESIDENCE WITH CENTRUM AT FORT WORDEN STATE PARK.
THIS BOOK IS COMPOSED IN FOURNIER, BY TYPEWORKS.

COPPER CANYON PRESS
Box 271, Port Townsend, Washington 98368

for Edouard Roditi

"The meanings in language are not original,
any more than the sounds;
They accrue from all the generations of human use."

–Robert Duncan

I

The Happy Poets

It's my delight to recite
my poems in the arms of

an intelligent girl and
to please her sweet ear

with what I have written.

Me iuvet in gremio doctae legisse puellae
auribus et puris scripta probasse mea
–PROPERTIUS II, xiii

And Goethe boasts that he
tapped out his hexameters

on the back of his Roman
girlfriend while she slept.

Und des Hexameters Mass leise mit fingern der Hand
Ihr auf den Rücken gezählt. Sie atmet in lieblichem Schlummer.
Und es durchglühet ihr Hauch mir bis ins Tiefste die Brust.
–GOETHE, *Römische Elegien* V

The Maker of Dreams

is his own master   he doesn't
take orders for who will be in

dreams (at least not in mine)
I've pleaded & reasoned with

him   I've explained to him
why you should be the star

in my dreams as often as pos-
sible because you are the one

for whom I'd been waiting so
long   he may be the maker of

dreams but you are the maker
of happiness   yet he is deaf

to my entreaties   he keeps
sending me persons of no in-

terest (such ordinary color-
less people) he should be

superseded as maker of dreams
either he has no taste or no

heart   I'm going to write to
the authorities to complain.

The Interdiction

You think you remember but
can you be certain you be-

lieve it happened but are
you sure were the things

said that each one heard
the other say were there

days were there nights did
it rain did the sun shine

it is forbidden to answer
any of these questions it

is forbidden to remember.

In the Ballet

I advance and extend my hand
you turn away and retreat (on

point)   we circle away from
each other as another couple

intervenes   when all four dance
together I'm able to take your

hand and you don't withdraw it
the others separate and drift

away   you mimic my clumsy move-
ments but now with affection

we must imagine the music and
how it draws us together till

our bodies are following each
other   you lead   I lead   we are

dancing as one   you don't re-
sist when I lift you in the air

and carry you across the stage
we must imagine the music   we

must imagine our pas de deux.

The Bird of Endless Time

Your fingers touch me like a bird's wing
like the feathers of the bird that returns

every hundred years to brush against a
peak in the Himalayas and not until the

rock's been worn away will time and the
kalpas end   why do I think of the fable

when I'm close with you   surely because
I want so many lives to feel your touch.

KALPA: *in Hinduism, an eon, a vast period of time that encompasses the creation and dissolution of a universe.*

The Kiss

In the films when the couples kiss
they grind their lips together as

if to prove their passion by break-
ing their teeth but your kiss was

barely a passing touch as delicate
as the breath of Zephyrus   I hardly

knew it had come before it was gone.

Somewhere in France

probably in a battered trunk
in the attic of a ruined châ-

teau is a bundle of papers
covered with faded handwrit-

ing I believe these to be
the chapters about women a-

bout his heroines which Stend-
hal could not print in his nov-

els because of the censorship
it is inconceivable that a

writer who could analyze the
mentations of love with such

sagacity would check his pen
when he got below the chin.

Blood

1953
Our best friends the Coopers who live across
Alameda near Mission have a dandy 10-year-old

daughter named Rosalynde   she's a peach and looks
like a peach good enough to eat but she's sort

of opinionated not a troublemaker but she knows
what's what   children pick up things at school

one day she comes home from school looking angry
what's the matter hon did Mrs. Balch get on your

back again about spelling   she doesn't say any-
thing she just goes into her room and turns up

the vic real loud (in those days they didn't have
hi-fis)   but at supper it comes out with a blast

listen you guys if you think I'm ever going to let
some man put his dirty thing inside me you've got

another think coming   no discussion she just goes
back into her room and turns up the music real high.

1965
We're not getting any younger as Harry says when he
slices one into the pond on 17 where the ducks are   no

we're not getting any younger we still live on Ala-
meda   we thought the second-hand Mercedes was a steal

but the bastard had turned back the odometer and the
repairs cost an arm & a leg   we are still pals with

Rosalynde but we don't see her too often   she has the
cutest little boutique down in Montecito with an apart-

ment over it   she sells stuff you can wear not that
nutty crap you see in *Vogue*   it's all a racket any-

way hems half way up to your ass one year and dragging
dirt off the floor the next   I still have a pretty de-

cent shape for my age   I have three outfits of nice slacks
and blouses for going out and just wear my jeans around all

day   (what was I talking about anyway?)   I know I shoot too
much breeze but Harry is sweet about it   he's the quiet type

but if he thinks of something to say to keep his end up he
just lights a cigarette which is unusual for him he doesn't

want to get lung cancer and I know it's time for me to but-
ton my lip   (oh yes Ros's husbands)   she married three times

and still looks great   none of her troubles were her fault
Wallace was killed in Korea (or maybe it was Vietnam I just

can't keep the dates straight on all that shit)   Thornton
was a nice guy but the booze got to him   he was a salesman

for Teentogs out of LA   you know three martinis with a good
customer at lunch and pretty soon one-two-three more when he

came home   Ros never knew when she could put on the
steak   she got him into AA but he didn't have the character to

stick with it   Wilbur is the damndest thing you ever heard
of   Harry thinks he's a spook   he was a professor of SocSci

at the U a real big brain   he told Ros he was flying to a con-
vention at Harvard only took an overnight bag & his briefcase

but he never came home   every now and then a pretty fat check
comes from some bank in Switzerland or the Cayman Islands but

never a call even on her birthday or Christmas   Harry thinks
he has gone underground to work for Colonel North   don't run

him down till they find the body Harry says he may end up a
national hero   Ros won't talk about it but I can tell she is

still in love with him   she had one girl from each husband all
peaches too   Pegeen (that's Irish) was named for me   Mirabel

is nutty about horses she's so good she gets paid to exercise
them   thank God she's too big to be a jockey   Ros Junior got

her brains from Wilbur   all "As" and editor of the paper at the
U   the serious type   she goes steady with a boy named Perkins

who writes poetry but it doesn't rhyme   some of it has been
printed in a literary magazine in Ojai   Harry and I both love

him he's so considerate with people   I don't mean sissy manners
he just seems to understand how a person is feeling but every

now and then Harry looks solemn and says there has got to be a
man-to-man talk about gainful employment   Ros Jr could be execu-

tive secretary for a big industrialist   she remembers things and
is always on the ball   but it's my hunch she's going to want to

have kids pretty soon   they wear helmets of course (that's the
state law) but I wish she would stop riding with him on his motor-

cycle   it wasn't his fault it was night and some drunk driving in
the middle of the road forced him into a tree   there were internal

injuries and it was nip & tuck in intensive care for several days
he had to have transfusions   and now there are these stories

on TV about how they don't always test properly   I wake
up in the night worrying about what may be in their blood.

Instructions

Empty your mind as completely
as you can and intone the sa-

cred words om mani padme hum
while you rub your left knee

with your right hand   believe
me as your spiritual director

I'm letting you off easy   in his
time Padma Sambhava would

have made you prostrate your-
self full length 500 times on

stony ground   you would have
been sanctified but black and

blue and very stiff for a week.

Mon Secret

Je demande qu'on me donne
un lit à l'hôpital des fous

figurez-vous comme j'ai souf-
fert dans ce beau monde tel

qu'il est   mon nom n'est pas
vraiment celui qui est in-

scrit sur ma carte d'identi-
té   personne ne sait qui je

suis (et je ne vais pas vous
le dire   c'est mon secret à

moi) j'attends de rencontrer
le Bon Dieu à l'hôpital des

fous   à Lui j'avouerai mon
vrai nom   il me reconnaîtra et

arrangera tout pour mon bien.

The Revenants

At a table in the corner two people
are talking in low voices a young

man and a girl they call each other
Paolo & Francesca if they are reven-

ants they are at least 800 years old
perhaps more (who knows there are

no birth certificates for revenants
or passports which limit where they

may go) they are speaking in an al-
most forgotten language seriously

quietly sadly as if once they had had
great sorrow (were they perhaps sepa-

rated in the lower world) sad chil-
dren of another time have they re-

turned here to find each other again
now and then the girl smiles for an

instant in a puzzled way he takes
her hand they go on talking softly.

. . . Nessun maggior dolore
Che ricordarsi del tempo felice
Ne la miseria. . .

–*Inferno,* v. 121–3

The Smallest Blessing

A cold wind freezes me inside
when I consider that someday

(perhaps not too long distant)
I won't be here to watch you

smile or listen to you laugh
or stroke you and touch you

where you love to be touched
I had such fears when I was a

child though there was little
reason for them (what had I to

lose then except my childish
self) but now when there's ev-

erything to lose that is love-
ly and excellent what can I

think what consolation can I
find   there's only the thought

that no one has ever been cer-
tain whether we know what we've

lost and long for its return.

The Cold

came suddenly & without warning
too swiftly for a wind to rise

or snow to fall   it seemed to
come from nowhere through clear

air (a gift from Canada or the
Arctic I suppose)   the sun was

powerless against it   our breath
steamed when we ventured out of

doors   the furnace groaned   the
fireplace swallowed logs   pipes

froze   cars wouldn't start   the
dogs wouldn't go out   the gros-

beaks deserted the feeder   three
days of frigeration   then finally

the sky clouded over & snow came
warming us like a blessed blanket.

Still Pond No More Moving

Let's not do anything in par-
ticular   let's not go anywhere

or see anyone   let's for an
hour or two just *be* (that is

exist) inhaling & exhaling in
the yoga fashion if you wish

but keeping our wits about us
so we can concentrate on each

other   who & what are you and
who am I and what is it that

makes us fit so well together?

The Enlacement

There's something holy about
falling asleep pressed close

against a beloved is it a sur-
vival from some primitive rite

it's more than the huddling
together of animals in the

storm is one body a sanctu-
ary for another the enlace-

ment's a vow for the future
a pledge not to be broken

now blood touches blood and
breath breath as if they were

hands touching and holding.

Rhyme

Isn't it good she asked (as
if there were no question in

the question) that we love
each other's bodies   one big

one small   one slim   one tall
isn't it good that we love the

way our skins taste the way
they feel to touch & stroke

of course I love you for your
mind and you me for my dispo-

sition but aren't we very lucky
our bodies love each other too?

The Hand Trick

She had a trick that she liked
to play with my hand (nothing

improper) it was a kind of tac-
tile hypnosis a stroking of my

fingers with the tips of hers
so that mine closed on my palm

by themselves and were reluctant
to open   it was a closure which

said to me I won't clutch you
but I don't want you to go away.

Le Hoqueton

Ne me confondez pas avec ce fripon
Eros   je suis hoqueton du roi je

lance mes flèches pour la gloire
(ou pour le butin) non pas pour l'am-

our   en effet les nénettes ne m'amu-
sent pas trop   pour la chasse je pré-

fére un cerf à douze bois ou un san-
glier saignant   le piquer cela en

vaut la peine   les femmes sont trop
molles et elles parlent après le fait.

The Unanswerable Question

It's easy to oblige you
when you say your whole

body wishes to be touching
all of mine from forehead

to feet   but what of the
soul   how can we realize

the soul   what is its lo-
cus   where does it reside?

The last two lines echo the language
of Pound's Cavalcanti translations

The Importance of Silence

Because there are some things
for which there are no names

there is no need for you to
try to invent them   your words

from the old poets are beauti-
ful to read on the page but the

ones I want to hear & feel come
from your lips and your hands.

In Half Darkness

your face is still so beautiful
there is a different radiance

that comes in sleep   I wake and
touch your cheek   I feel your

breath on my groping fingers
your eyes are closed but I sus-

pect they can see & are watch-
ing what is to come   they are

looking into the future as far
as the end of our time together.

II

The Escape

The world is too much with us
let's float away from it   I

don't mean death (which may
be an illusion) but an écarte-

ment (a separation) a ver-
fremdung (an estrangement)

we shall agree to withdraw
not into the great nothing-

ness as a Buddhist might do
but into each other (your

being would set my limits &
mine yours) can we try to be-

come invisible except to our-
selves and learn a language

that only we need understand?

Die Heimat

He had walked so far to find her
through uplands over rough and

rocky roads   when in the end he
came to her at first he didn't

reckon where he was   he'd never
been in that country   the ter-

rain was not like anything he'd
seen   it took him many months

to understand this was his home.

An Anginal Equivalent

For those little stabs of pain
in the region of the heart the

poet is having an EKG   the wires
are attached to a small TV and

as he lies there he can watch
the bouncing beat on the screen

qualim asks Martial velim quae-
ris nolimve puellam? nolo nimis

facilem difficilemque nimis what
does that jerking line tell him

about the prospect for his new
affection illud quod medium est

atque inter utrumque probamus
nec volo quod cruciat nec volo

quod satiat which will she be?

You ask what kinds of girl I like and don't like
Let her not be a pushover, yet not too hard to get
Somewhere between the two
Not one who tears me to pieces
But not one who hangs on my neck.
—MARTIAL I, lvii

Elusive Time

In love it may be dangerous
to reckon on time to count

on it   time's here and then
it's gone   I'm not thinking

of death or disaster but of
the slippage the unpredicted

disappearance of days on which
we were depending for happiness.

It Can Happen

Was it too quick to be true
was it Eros who shot two ar-

rows   it was almost as swift
as if some god had flicked a

switch and love came on like
light   amor lux est said An-

dalasius   c'était un coup de
foudre disait Ariane d'Haute-

ville and in Hamburg ganz wie
ein blitz (Herr Bosenkamp) oh

it can happen   so blessed be
Eros (or whomever it was) that

it could happen even to me.

L'Avertissement

Que serait été ma vie si tu
n'avait pas osé me donner ce

jour-là le signal tout secret
de ton égard   par les conven-

ances une jeune fille bien é-
levée comme toi (et surtout de

race) ne montre aucune prédi-
lection intime (surtout pour

un rustaud comme moi)   ten-
aillé mais timide je te re-

gardais de loin te parlant
seulement avec les yeux a-

baissés ne pensant pas que
tu puisses me priser à titre

particulier   quelle joie et
quelle surprise alors quand

tu m'indiqua avec une finesse
si délicate que tu saurait m'ac-

corder un coin dans ton coeur
un coin petit mais tout à moi.

By The Numbers

What number do you start with
when you count   let's dream of

another life   idiot savants do
fantastic feats with numbers

but they don't know how they
do them   let's dream of ano-

ther life   Rexroth explained
Godel's Proof to me that time

when we were camping in King's
River Canyon but it's gone from

my head now like so many other
things   let's dream of another

life   I prefer an abacus to a
computer   let's dream of ano-

ther life   in Sikkim a thous-
and prostrations each day and

a thousand iterations of the
mantra of the jewel at the

heart of the lotus   so let us
now praise other lives and

hope that we may count them.

The Problem Struck Me

when the crew from the tele-
phone company came to replace

a pole out on the road   I ask-
ed them which is the better an

old post in a new hole or a
new post in an old hole   one

of them whirled his finger a-
round his ear the way one does

with a crazy but the other man
put down his shovel & started

to think   it's the kind of prob-
lem which occupied the scholas-

tics (they must have had a lot
of time on their hands when they

weren't coaxing angels to dance
on the heads of pins) he didn't

say anything but I could tell
I'd gotten to him   I hope he

won't do anything rash like ask-
ing his supervisor at the tele-

phone company or even throwing
up his job   chances are he has

a wife & kids and needs the money
more than a life of speculation.

[with Andrew Crozier]

The Beautiful One

Vojo the night elevator man
the old fellow from Zagreb

is much concerned about you
it's clear that you're his

favorite in the building (he
calls you najlepšsa the beauti-

ful one like the youngest of
the three princesses in the

fairy tale) but he says you
don't go out enough how she

get husband when she sit up
there all time reading books

she have to go dancing to get
husband is what old Vojo says

The Drawing Lesson

The student is sketching a nude girl
who is trying to bite the big toe on

her left foot   or is she trying to
kiss her toe as she sits there on

the bed twisting her leg into a po-
sition like an exercise in Yoga   it

must be terribly uncomfortable even
painful   a little child could do it

but a grown person would have to be
double-jointed   the student pauses

in his drawing to study her face for
a clue that might explain her action

but her expression reveals nothing
no smile no sign of anger   all he

can see in her face is concentration
she wants to bite (or kiss?) her toe.

The Golden Years

I belong to the American Association
of Retired People and get 10% off at

the hardware store but not at the li-
quor store   it was a close call with

my driving license renewal   in the
parking test I backed over the curb

but he was a nice guy and let me try
it again   Calendula (the cook) says

the *back* of my head is still handsome
and at my last physical Dr Chen put

on my chart that my weight had not in-
creased but was simply redistributed

I'm waiting for my cataracts to ripen.

Our Bicycles

At Versailles only the Queen may have pompons on her coach-covers; fastened with nails, and of any colour that she pleases. Duchesses have blue covers. Wives of eldest sons of dukes have red covers. Widows have black velvet.

–The Duc de Saint-Simon
Historical Memoirs

My brother being the eldest had
for his bike the most elaborate

accoutrements   a pair of squirrel
tails (one grey one brown) which

flew from his handlebars   Cousin
Ham had an extra gear for attack-

ing the hills of Shadyside where
we lived   Cousin Georgie (the shy

one) had two bells with different
tones but when he took his hands

off the bars trying to sound both
of them at once his front wheel

swerved and he ended up at the
hospital for 4 stitches   as for

me (the youngest) I was still on
a tricycle and had nothing but

tears when the others sped on a-
head of me (wait for me wait for

me I would cry) leaving me far be-
hind wailing and eating their dust.

Our Meetings

Where do our thoughts meet
after we have sent them to

each other down the sidere-
al pathways   will they come

together again at Vrindavan
where Radha and the blue god

Krishna loved & are loving

> Let the earth of my body be mixed
> with the earth my beloved walks on
> Let the fire of my body be the brightness
> in the mirror that reflects his face
> Let the water of my body join the waters
> of the lotus pool he bathes in

will they meet again on the
black ship where Tristan and

la belle Iseut sang mournfully

> Sehnender Minne
> schwellendes Blühen
> schmachtender Liebe
> seliges Glühen
> Jach in der Brust
> jauchzende Lust

or in the castle of Montagnac
above the Vezère where En Ber-

tran pursued the fair Maheut

Domna puois de me no-us chal
e partit m'avetz de vos
sens totas ochaisos
no sai on m'enquieira
que ja mais
non er per me tan rics jais
cobratz e si del semblan
no trop domna a mon talan
que valha vos qu'ai perduda
ja mais no vuolh aver druda

Our thoughts have met at many
times in many places through

divers bodies have we joined
our thoughts so often before

now have we lived this love.

The translation from the Bengali of Radha's hymn to Krishna is from Levertov & Dimock: *In Praise of Krishna.*

The duet in German is from Act 1, Scene 5 of Wagner's libretto for *Tristan and Isolde.*

Passionate longing-song
Swelling and blooming
Languishing love
glow of high bliss
deep in the heart
jubilant desire. . .

Bertrand de Born's compleynte when Maheut de Montagnac has given him the gate follows the text of Roubaud's anthology, *Les Troubadours.*

Lady, since you no longer care for me
and have sent me away for no reason
I don't know where to look for love
because never will there be such rich joy for me
or ever found again in your likeness
Since there cannot be a lady the equal
of the one I've lost
I never want to have a lover again.

I Love to See You

in the box of paperclips on my desk
it's a good place for you because I

can look at you when I'm telephoning
or typing a poem or putting poems in-

to the copy machine to send to maga-
zines that don't want them   I tried

putting you in the little ormolu
frame where the daguerreotype of

great-grandmother Henrietta used to
be but it didn't suit   you looked

too formal (you have lovely manners
but thank heaven you aren't formal)

so I pushed up the paperclips in the
box and leaned you against the heap

it can't be very comfortable (paper-
clips are harder than hay) but you're

smiling away as if you loved it   I
hope you're also smiling because you

love me so much you don't care where
I keep you even in the paperclip box.

Her Reply

I like my picture to be in the box
where you keep your paperclips   I

imagine that when you reach for a
clip you are reaching out for me

it's a gesture you've made a thou-
sand times (whenever you've needed

a clip) but now I hope it has be-
come different   given a new mean-

ing by my image   does the movement
of your hand now plead more for me

than thought or memory can   even
at this distance I feel the touch

of your fingers   do they feel they
are touching me   or must I become

again only the icon of my everyday
self as ordinary as your paperclips?

The Waiters' Ballet

At the Grand Véfours in the Palais Royal
the waiters have obviously been trained

in ballet as well as religious ritual
they bow they hover they flutter they

are always smiling respectfully they
dance attendance when they serve a

dish   their hands move like mudras or
the gestures at the altar in the mass

as they approach the table there is a
slight genuflection in one knee   when

they pour the wine it is a sacred cere-
mony   between servings they never take

their eyes off the tables in case some
request may be communicated to them with

an eyebrow   an exquisite performance but
what do they say among themselves after

the guests have gone (apart of course from
discussing the tips) that's what I wonder.

The Inviolable Maiden

Came she not from the pages of Malory, from the *Morte Darthur?*
Was she not of the line of Morgan le Fay—but sans covin or mal
engine, without the malice of Morgan?

A magical maiden, bewitched and bewitching, casting spell on
the knights,
Sir Turquine, Sir Mordaunt, Sir Uwaine le Blanchemains, Sir
Persides de Bloise and many another.
But their hands have left no mark upon her,
Their lips have not touched her lips,
She is not of the night but of the morning,
She need not lave her limbs in the mere sith they have not been
distained.
The inviolable maiden, nesh and unstained.
No man has entered her though many have sought to slip her.
The force of men is powerless against her, their violence is vain;
Her virtue is proof against all attainment,
The maiden inviolate.

Child of a sorceress but she is as pure in heart as she is perfect in
body;
No man hath halsed her, no wile can defile her.
At dawn they have seen her in the brackenland, sometimes
amounted on a white palfrey, but none have caught or
taken her;
She is too swift in flight for the hounds or the harriers,
The inviolable maiden, no man hath ta'en her.

As dusk they have seen her on the moorland or by the sea cliffs
but she has always escaped them;

She is never there when they come to the place where they have espied her.
The bracken may be defoiled as if a roe deer had slept in it but she is nowhere to be found.
She is invisible when the halfmoon rises over the menhirs.

δραπέτευσε σκύλος μεγαι και μικραι drapeteuse skylos megai kai mikrai, again and again she escapes the knights, they cannot take her with great hounds nor brachets.

παρθένος απαραβιαστος parthenos aparabiastos, the inviolable maiden.
No man hath felt her breath on his cheek,
No man hath tasted her spittle;
No man's tongue has travelled her mouth.
No man can swear he hath heard her speak,
No man hath distained her nor brought her to disworship.
All they have heard was the wind soughing, the wind making compleynt for their dole,
The swough of the wind dying.

παρθένος απαραβιαστος parthenos aparabiastos, the maiden inviolate.

μάγισσα εμέ κινοῦμαι magissa eme kinoumai, she hath me ensorcelled, and many before me,
I am weak from her beauty, as many before me;
My valor avails not.

I was enslaved on the moorland by the sweet smile of that maiden,
I fell in the bracken, my corselet to-shivered by the lance of her glance.
I am bewitched by the inviolable maiden—but not malfortuned.

GLOSSARY (from that of the Medici Society edition of *Le Morte Darthur*)

attaint : overcome
brachet : little hound
clip : embrace
covin : deceit
distain : sully
disworship : shame
dole : sorrow
espied : seen
halsed : embraced
mal engine : evil design
malfortune : ill-luck
nesh : soft, tender
sith : since
slip : embrace
swough : sound of wind
to-shivered : broken to pieces

EDITOR'S NOTE: It is apparent that the knights were not well instructed in Greek.

A Parable

Once upon a time when I
was about eight Papa took

me with him to lunch at
the house of Mrs R   she

was very beautiful and
gave me two helpings

of ice cream   after lunch
Papa told me to go out in-

to the yard to play   I
climbed a tree and look-

ed in a window   Papa and
Mrs R were doing strange

things   they were lying on
the bed and had no clothes

on   this was a long time
ago but I still see them

there doing strange things.

A Parenthesis

(This poet defaces his couplets with parentheses
[a word from the Greek coming from para (beside)

+ en (in) + tithenai (to put) whence to put in be-
side] this is a practice très mal vu (deplored)

by ergoistical critics who point out that his
lines would be grammatically more correct with

commas or colons   the poet responds quite true
but would they still be mine   for him the paren-

theses are small fortresses in which he can take
refuge from logic and conventional behavior   his

psychiatrist has a more sinister reading on the
(s) [are their shapes not bivulvar] but he holds

his peace since they content his bizarre patient.

A Translation

How did you decide to translate me
from one language to another   let's

say from the English of friendship
to the French of lovers   we'd known

each other half a year when one day
as we were talking (it was about one

of your drawings) suddenly you curl-
ed yourself against me and drew my

lips down to yours   it was so deft
an alternance from one language to

the other as if to say yes you can
speak French to me now if you wish.

After Hardy

The time-torn man had waited
long for your coming even des-

pairing that could be (how
might he find such fortune?)

then when at last you came
(illumined as you are) when

the hope-hour stroked for him
he touched your hand (dread-

ing it would turn to shadow)
declared he was sewn by it

(the tear sewn) and was no
longer in his fear of time.

– FROM HARDY
A Broken Appointment

Am I Not Lucky

that you decided to love me
what if you wanted to love

a cat or a dog or dresses
or even Paul Newman   I've

never quite understood how
it happened   I was having my

life you yours and each
seemed content   we knew each

other slightly but only as
friends   then suddenly with-

out warning or expectation
you decided to love me (and

I you) & my life was changed.

At the Boule D'Or

As they lunch together at
the Boule d'Or they are

smiling a lot and choosing
their words carefully   this

is their first date & each
is trying to impress   they

are feeling each other out
and weighing the potentials

(her beauty & his capacity
for making money)   now they

are laughing & talking with
more animation   they find

they like each other   but
can either foresee the bit-

ter words that will follow?

Ein Kleines Herzlied

Du bist in mein Herz plötz-
lich gekommen   lass mich bet'

ich in deinem stehen   einsam
trat ich im Lebenswege bis

dass du mich vornahmst zu dreh-
en in andere Strassen die in

einen Garten leiten wo findest
du dich und endlose Schönheiten.

The Blue Footprints

Some nights along the sidewalks
in our neighborhood someone is

making blue footprints   they
must do it with a stencil per-

haps attached to a stick   they
must carry a pot of paint be-

cause the prints are very clear
and not smudged   the prints will

begin in the middle of a block
go around a corner or two and

then stop   I can think of no
reason why they begin and end

where they do   it's a joke of
course but a very laborious

one   hundreds of carefully made
footprints   after a few days

the prints fade out but then
they are made again though

not always made in the same
place   I have been out late

at night to catch the mysteri-
ous walker but have not found

him I've asked the patrolmen
in the police car but they have

seen nothing they just laugh
they say the footprints are

not a hazard but they worry
me they upset me I want to

know where they are going
and what their message is.

Danger / Road Under Repair

Something was being done to the road
through our village and to the course

of our lives   it wasn't clear what au-
thority had ordered these changes   one

day workmen we didn't know appeared
(they were from another province we

couldn't understand their dialect) and
began to improve a thoroughfare which

had been satisfactory for longer than
anyone could remember   it was more than

filling a few potholes after a hard win-
ter   it was a complete rebuilding   even

some jogs in the road were to be straight-
ened out   first we were puzzled as we saw

the work proceed then alarmed   we knew
there was nothing wrong with our road

why were these changes being made
what unknown power had ordained them?

III

The Invitation

They were lolling on the couch
talking about nothing much   they

were holding hands and kissing
in a desultory way   she was wear-

ing a white silk dress   when he
raised it he found she had on

nothing underneath   she had want-
ed him to find his way with ease.

Ever So

Past midnight & I
was awakened by the

screaming of some
small animal in

the woods beyond
the farther side of

the sheep pasture
so long an agony

I fell back to sleep
again before it was

ended   and who
was pursued who

the pursuer   I my-
self might be the

one or the other.

Mei Axis Mundi

You are the center about
which my being revolves

you are the intersection
of every possible line

I cannot describe you ex-
cept to say you are Sumeru

and Taishan you are the
point of rest from which

comes all that is light.

The Ritual

The ritual of the poem in praise of you
demands the vision of a goddess   an ap-

parition   an evocation   the goddess may
be the Cytherean born of the seafoam

she of dark eyelids   venerandam   or she
of the moon & the grove   her nymphs ga-

thered about her   choros nympharum   ven-
erandam   or she who sprang from the head

of her father   blue-eyed glaukopis mo-
ther of cities   venerandam   there are

other goddesses in the Hymni Deorum who
are of great beauty and clairvoyance but

I cannot choose for you among them   you
alone can reveal to me your hidden name.

A Sweet Kiss

When I was little and had
been bad when the back of

the hairbrush had been ap-
plied as I kicked & scream-

ed when the tears of repen-
tance had been shed I would

ask my mother for a "sweet
kiss" it was a special kind

of kiss a moist slightly sal-
ty kiss because she too had

been crying as she punished me.

Such Grace

is in her step   such grace
goes in the movement of her

arms & shoulders as she walks
such grace in how she holds

her head   how graceful the
gestures of her hands   such

grace in the way she slightly
tilts her face toward me when

a smile is beginning there
the float in air of a dan-

cer   suspended flight of a
hummingbird   always she goes

in grace   there is such
grace in all her going.

Mes Souffrances

Je souffre parce que je suis
laid et elle est si belle   je

suis presqu' aveugle et elle
voit tout si clair   je marche

à quatre pattes et elle vole
comme une hirondelle   je me mords

la langue quand je parle mais
elle chante comme le rossignol

mes souffrances sont intolér-
ables mais quand elle me jête

un sourire je les oublie toutes.

The First Night

we spent together was like
school each was trying to

teach the other what was
liked or not liked the de-

tails are irrelevant what
mattered was that love was

becoming a real thing be-
tween us without regard to

this or that preference.

Floating Free

She wanted to float free
no ropes no pins no nails

no wires nothing holding
her too tightly to some-

thing nothing binding her
too closely to another per-

son enough space around her
enough of her own quiet e-

nough open light   on the
water or in the air any-

where at all that she might
be she wanted to float free.

Prolepsis

You are a future, my poor darling, that pretends to be a past but will never be a present.
—FROM STENDHAL'S *Lucien Leuwen*

I always feared that things
would end badly between us

but never imagined how you
would humiliate me at a mo-

ment when my passion for you
was at its peak
                    One of your
attractions (if I can call

it that) was your temper   if
you were bored or displeas-

ed how your eyes flashed
how your language whipped

my skin
          In the bedroom of
the hotel in Luzern after

you had had your bath you
paraded before the mirrors

with only a towel wrapped
around your head as if it

were a turban in a harem.

Les Patineurs

s'en vont traînant leurs chevilles
comme ballades   ils glissent vers

le nirvana du froid   une jambe deux
jambes des pieds sans nombre   flic

flac et droulala   (ne répondant pas
aux sifflets du vent)   mais les pa-

tineurs n'arrivent pas à m'arracher
des coulisses noires   pas de soleil

aucune lumière   je me sens englouti
sous la glace solide   hors d'haleine

mon sang se congèle   resterai-je dans
cet abîme   les patineurs sont si loin.

The Offering

He was reaching out to her
offering the best of his

old beaten-up furniture
from the rooms where so

many disappointments had
been enacted so many ri-

diculous little comedies
of frustration and folly

yes it would all be dif-
ferent now (he promised

her that) because they
would be her things too.

It's Indelicate

I know to bore you with tales
of old loves   you must deter

me if you find these ladies
unappetizing but love is cumu-

lative and each one of them is
still a little piece of me as

I am still (I hope) a part of
them   no cause for jealousy

each had her time each had my
time of me but now those times

are past and have become only
a moment of obscure propinquity.

Her Letters

Did he imagine that her letters
were written to him those ones

which described in such detail
the topography of her heart (though

always in phrases whose chaleur
did not exceed what was permis-

ible to a lady of breeding and
discretion) didn't he know she

was writing to someone who did
not exist or at least no longer

existed for her because she was
tired of him oh so bored with

him but didn't know how to break
off   and so he had become a phan-

tom it being her disposition to
write to a lover alive or dead.

Elle n'en continuait pas moins à lui ecrire des lettres amoureuses, en vertu de cette idée qu'une femme doit toujours écrire à son amant.

Mais, en écrivant, elle percevait un autre homme, un fantôme fait de ses plus ardents souvenirs . . .

—EMMA'S LETTERS TO LÉON
Madame Bovary

The Long Night

He lies alone in his bed
listening to the dry high-

pitched sound of the ci-
cadas singing because it

is night when they awaken
in the dark   their reso-

nation means nothing to
him it is familiar he has

heard it too many times
before   likely enough it

will be several hours be-
fore he can fall asleep

again   his eyes are too
tired for reading   the

words blur when he turns
on the light to resume

his book (it's a life of
that clever woman Madame

de Maintenon how she be-
guiled and dominated the

Sun King) like the cicadas
the story means little to

him it is the blur & buzz
of lives lived long ago

lives that might just as
well never have happened

for all the thought he can
give to them now   he ima-

gines that somehow he is
inside the cicadas that he

is helping them make their
sound   he resents this im-

prisonment but cannot es-
cape from it   he fears that

he will never be able to
hear any other sound that

there will be no sleep but
most he resents that he can-

not understand the meaning
of the sound he is making.

The Inn at Kirchstetten

Notes Pencilled in the Margins of a Book of the *Dichtungen* of Georg Trakl

How can I thank you B, for your ear, your mind, your affection? Some afternoons after we had given kisses we would recline against the hard bolsters in the little inn reading and rewriting my poems.

At first the idea of exchanging caresses with an almost heavenly being had frightened me. I committed little crimes so you would postpone this perilous happiness.

No one had told me that it was possible to make love to a voice.

Only someone who has not shared such love will condemn these writings.

The toy train which brought us to the town was so slow. It stopped at every hamlet. Farm people got on and off. There was a car for their animals: lambs, pigs, chickens. When it was very slow we would become frantic with impatience. We had so little time to be together.

Outside the window of the inn were the streets of the town, its old houses. But if we watched hard enough the scene would change into a landscape of fields, trees, a little lake and mountains in the distance.

Horses went clip-clop down the cobbled street. It was a blessing there were so few autos and motorbikes.

There was a gilt-framed mirror on the wall of the room. Why did we see in it the reflection of only one person?

The sound of rain on the window. The sound of the wind. The sound of the sun. Yes, even sunlight has its sound though only lovers are likely to hear it.

You were disgusted by the big cockroaches that scuttled across the floor until I convinced you they carried secret messages. Our postmen.

I always brought flowers to talk when love had rendered us silent.

Sometimes you would say, I can't remember who we are. I have to look at the shoes on the carpet to recall our names.

A strange ballet. The horizontal pas de deux. Hands mimicking the dancers' feet. Your long hair is your costume?

A bird struck the window with a thud and fell into the street. It was eager to join us but couldn't see the glass.

We read no more that day. There was nothing the book could tell us. Paolo and Francesca, you said. We often heard faint footsteps in the hall, not as heavy as those of the inn servants. You said it was the revenants who wanted to be with us. You opened the door but no one was there.

The inn servants seemed an honest lot but it was just as well to tip them a bit too much. I used the name Reseguier but you might have been recognized from your pictures in the magazines.

There were porcelain basins and pitchers, two of each, on the stand and eider puffs on the bed, two fat white pancakes on the matrimonial.

There was a picture on the wall which I couldn't place, most unusual for a village inn, not a religious or hunting scene. It was an abstract drawing in several colors. A grid of little nearly identical shapes connected by ink lines. Perhaps an artist from the city hadn't been able to pay his bill.

Sometimes, if you dozed, I would change the time on your watch that you always put on the bedside stand. I knew you would wake with a start and say it was time to go home, he would be waiting for your company at tea. There were later trains on the toy railroad.

Hot and cold weather, we went there for nearly a year. Who is using that room now? Perhaps a series of lonely travelling salesmen.

You must know that none of these things may ever have happened, that we imagined them. . . . How can we be sure it was not all an illusion? Remember the wineglass you dropped and it shattered? We tried to get up all the crumbs of glass but some were too small and worked their way into the fabric of the carpet. They would prove we were there.

Editor's Note

The book of Trakl was found in 1983 in a secondhand shop near the Stefanskirche in Vienna. The marginal markings, which are written vertically, are in two hands, one male, one female. The neat male hand is in the old

German handschrift. The female hand is more difficult to read, a mixture of Romanic and Cyrillic letters. Perhaps from Moldavia?

Neither B nor her lover have been identified. The bookseller in Vienna could not recall where the Trakl had come from. From the description of the "toy train" the town may have been Kirchstetten, where W.H. Auden was later to have his summer home, and the inn the Drei Falken.

In the Salzkammergut

What did you do with my heart
after I'd lent it to you   did

you leave it in the Salzkammer-
gut somewhere near Koos's house

(the one that is built on stilts
in the water of the Ammer See) I

went back to look for it there
but never a trace   and none of

the peasants remembered Marili
or Annalise   totally disappear-

ed   will it be the same with you?

KOOS: *J.J. Van der Leeuw, the Dutch philosopher and theosophist, author of* The Fire of Creation *and* Gods in Exile. *In H.D.'s* Tribute to Freud, *Van der Leeuw is the man whom H.D. often met coming down the stairway at Berggasse 19. His wealth came from his family's plantations in Sumatra. He was killed when he tried to fly solo from Vienna to Capetown and crashed in the Atlas.*

It's March

and the sap is running in
the sugar maples   the chil-

dren from the brotherhood
are collecting the sap buck-

ets in our woodlot   it's an
outing for them and they're

laughing and shouting most
merrily   there's still a

foot of snow so it's hard
going for some of the lit-

tle ones to drag the buck-
ets to the tank wagon with-

out spilling them   the old
horse who pulls the wagon

droops his head he's bored
he longs to get back to the

stable for his feed   the chil-
dren from the brotherhood wear

old-fashioned clothes but in
bright colors mostly blues &

reds it's a scene from Brueghel.

Poets

It is the nature of poets
to believe that they are

great (or will become great)
that their lines will echo

down the ages and be studied
by schoolchildren   but this

is statistically unlikely
the latest figures from the

NEA estimate that there are
about 100,000 more or less

literate poets in the USA
(of whom 10% are graduates

of creative writing courses)
I think my favorite of all

these poets is a young man
I met in Santa Fe   he played

the role of a poet because he
felt like a poet but he never

took the risk of writing a
single poem   his life was

his poetry and he was happy.

The Unenlightened Face

The Buddhists speak of an Unenlightened
Face   the face of one who has not yet

found the light   as I walk I turn my
face toward the sun   I feel its warmth

but the light has not yet entered me
perhaps the light must come from what

was written   what was told by those
who sat beside him long ago   I read

the texts but the light does not enter
me   I know it is not given to all to

receive the light no matter how they
may long for it   perhaps I'm one of

the darkfaced the sons of attachment.

Thumbs Up!

What if we were not enantio-
morphic if our thumbs were

both on the same side of our
hands (and the big toes the

same of course) would our e-
volution have been different

would we have made our home
underground instead of in

the trees (because matching
thumbs could dig better than

climb) in ten million years
there were endless possibil-

ities don't think about them
they might still come true.

The Sorrows of Smindyrides

He is a delicate flower indeed
talk of the princess and the pea

Aelianus recounts that the syba-
rite Smindyrides spent a sleep-

less night because one of the
rose petals strewn on his bed

was folded in two (his slave
the unfortunate folder of pe-

tals was severely beaten) my
friend delights in pulverizing

reputations but if he is criti-
cized for misplacing a comma his

dinner is gall in his mouth and
his wine too bitter to swallow.

Les Chimères de Sainte-Hélène

Dans ses derniers jours (gardant son sérieux) il m'explique
qu'aucun médecin n'avait jamais trouvé avec un
stéthoscope le battement de son coeur
"N'est-il pas vrai," demanda-t-il, "qu'on est heureux d'être
égoïste et insensible?"
A Gourgaud il constata, "Je voyais toujours les choses tellement
en masse et de si haut que les hommes s'échappaient à
ma vue."
Un beau matin on l'a soulevé de son lit (il était maintenant assez
gros) et on l'a fait s'asseoir dans un fauteuil auprès de la
fenêtre. Pour un instant il souriait. "Bonjour soleil;
bonjour mon ami."
Ses yeux s'affaiblissaient. Il me pria de lui lire à haute voix les
vers de Voltaire:
"Mais à revoir Paris, je ne dois plus prétendre,
Vous voyez qu'au tombeau je suis prêt à descendre."
Une nuit quand je veillais à son lit je l'entendais chuchoter en
délire, "Mon fils, un jour tu seras à la tête de la Grande
Armée."
Les mots se confondent dans les livres. La vitre s'est obscurcie.
Mais nous savons qu'avant Thèbes et Oedipe les dieux ont déjà
su construire des monstres sacrés.

(Collage from AUBRY: *Sainte-Hélène;* ROSEBURY: *Napoleon, the Last Phase;* FORSYTH: *History of the Captivity of Napoleon at St Helena;* BRICE: *Les Espoirs de Napoléon à Sainte-Hélène;* BERTRAND: *Cahiers de Sainte-Hélène;* FIRMIN-DIDOT: *La Captivité de Sainte-Hélène;* THOMPSON: *Napoleon Bonaparte.)*

At Benares

the saintly yogi Hari-Hara-Baba
who lived on a boat beside the

ghats of the Ganges where he re-
ceived his devotees completely

naked had to be rowed to the other
side of the river twice daily be-

cause he had made a vow never to
soil the most sacred part of the

riverbank where the bodies of the
dead are consumed in fires of san-

dalwood with his impure excrement.

—FROM ALAIN DANIELOU
The Way of the Labyrinth

The Limper

Rilke writes of the expectation
that a beloved is about to ap-

pear   but in what form will she
come   as a living person or an

apparition   and how will we re-
cognize each other   what sign

will there be that she is the
chosen one   in my case I hope

she has been warned about my
limp   no one can fail to no-

tice it   my limp is well known
throughout the city   they call

me the limper   some think my
limp is good luck and some

bad   I know people talk about
it   she will know me by my

limp and will speak to me.

"Warst du nicht immer
noch von Erwartung zerstreut, als kündigte alles
eine Geliebte dir an?"

–*Duineser Elegien,* I, 31–33

A Book about Nothing

was what he wanted to write
what claim had he to express

any opinions   there must be
no sign of himself in such a

book   since everything he be-
lieved was probably wrong why

bother to put it down   no story
and no characters just nothing

no romance & no speculation
just nothing   he had to stop

using words because they kept
trying to turn themselves into

ideas (or one word would beget
the next word like cells repro-

ducing) in the end he covered
his paper with lines of periods

& dashes then he took out the
dashes they were too distract-

ing   so his book of nothing had
only dots   at last he was happy

he had composed his masterpiece.

These verses take off from bits of Flaubert's correspondence. On 16 January 1852 he wrote to his impossible girlfriend Louise Colet: "Ce qui me semble beau, ce que je voudrais faire, c'est un livre sur rien, un livre sans attache extérieure. . . " and on 8 February 1852 he told her that he didn't want there to be a single authorial comment. To his great friend George Sand he wrote on 5 December 1866: "Je trouve même qu'un romancier n'a pas le droit d'exprimer son opinion *sur quoi que ce soit. Est-ce que le bon Dieu l'a jamais dite, son opinion?"*

The Endless Mirrors

In the Gonzaga Palace in Mantua
(which has more than 800 rooms)

there is a great hall whose four
walls (except for the one with

windows) are entirely covered
with mirrors so that wherever

you stand you see yourself end-
lessly reflected each mirror re-

peating the image in the one op-
posite though each reflection is

diminished in size   standing in
that room I see myself getting

smaller and smaller until in the
end there is only a figure so

minuscule I can no longer recog-
nize it as myself and cannot even

be certain I really exist at all.

The Atman of Sleep

You had fallen asleep beside
me and your closed eyes in

the dusklight were so beauti-
ful   the fingers of one hand

were curled like a child's a-
gainst your cheek   I listened

for the cadence of your breathing
and made mine come & go with

yours one breath for both of us.

A Graceful Exit

Was it difficult to escape
from those novels of Henry

James   Isabel Archer   Mag-
gie Verver   Millie Theale

which one were you   a bit
of each I think (but none

of that little idiot Daisy
Miller)   something from each

to make up the way you are
the quiet style (since you

were in his head tell me
how much of that is from

his style) grace in behavior
grace in the movements

of mind and speech   such
delicacy of perception   a

special kind of kindness
when did it come to you

that you must leave the
books   was it done for me?

Thirteen Ways of Looking at a Lovebird

"A man and a woman
Are one.
A man and a woman and a blackbird
Are one."

–Wallace Stevens
"Thirteen Ways of Looking at a Blackbird"

"It is better to marry than to burn."

–St. Paul

i It is difficult to be rational about love.
ii In love actions are ruled by emotions.
iii Actions in love are determined by forces which are mysterious.
iv Logic retreats before sentiment.
v It can be more important to win a kiss than material advantage.
vi The advice of friends is usually useless in solving problems of the heart.
vii Most books on love are written in foreign languages.
viii In love the role of time is perplexing.
ix There is short love and there is long love.
x There is also love without love.
xi Love is a game of true and false.
xii It is also a game of chance.
xiii But it is better to win than to lose.

Then and Now

The Rain

is speaking it pelts
against the windows
and on the roof
in the night
it makes thousands
of little words
which confuse the child
who does not understand
such a language
what is the rain
trying to tell him
should he be afraid
is there a message
of danger to be escaped
or can he be lulled
by the sound of the rain
and go back to sleep?

The Poem

is moving by itself
it proceeds of its
own accord
the writer of the poem
has no idea where
it will lead him
he cannot control it
because it has
its own life
separate from his own
what if it carries him off
from his safe life
from his accustomed loves
should he fear harm
from the poem and tear up
the page or simply put it
aside and go back to sleep?

Hope Springs

Do you think he likes me   I have
the feeling it's going to start

anytime now   we have our desks
a few rows apart in Customers'

Complaints   a week ago when I
glanced over his way he smiled

at me   then the next day he fol-
lowed me to the water fountain

all he said was the old bitch
(meaning Mrs McIlhenny) sure is

laying it on us these days isn't
she   but he was looking me over

I'm going to Bloomie's to price
one of those cashmere sweaters

that were in their ad   maybe if
I sit by myself in the cafeteria

not with the girls he'll come to
join me   he looks a little like

Al Pacino in Serpico but I can
tell he's sweet and even if he's

stuck in Customers' Complaints
I'll bet he's smart I think it's

going to begin any day now.

The Big Clock

She fell in love with the face
of a clock the big one in the

tower of the Woolworth Building
it all began one day when she

stopped to rest on a bench in
Union Square   she got the notion

the clock was talking to her and
when the big hand moved with a

jerk from one minute to the next
she felt it wanted to touch her

cheek   it was love at three o'clock
she changed jobs to an office on the

west side of the square where she
could watch the clock   any sunny

day you can find her on the bench
with her paper bag lunch making

love with her eyes to the big clock.

God Bless America!

She is walking home from the post
office with her arms full of pack-

ages   she is smiling   she looks so
happy   what are all those things

she ordered from catalogs? toys for
the kids? a gadget for the kitchen?

a new blouse for herself? I think
she has more reason to feel pleased

than she may realize   she is sus-
taining the economy   even if she

gets behind now & then she's in-
creasing the gross national pro-

duct   she's doing something about
unemployment   God bless her for

all that and God bless America!

My Ambition

is to become a footnote
in a learned work of the

22nd century   not just a
"cf" or a "see" but a sol-

id note such as Raby gives
Walafrid Strabo in *Christ-*

ian Latin Poetry or Ernst
Robert Curtius (the most

erudite German who ever
lived) devotes to Alber-

tino Mussato in his *Euro-*
päische Literatur und La-

teinisches Mittelalter   I
hope the scholar of the

22nd will lick his schol-
arly lips when he finds me

in some forgotten source
(perhaps the *Obloquies* of

Dreadful Edward Dahlberg)
and think here is an odd-

ball I would have liked
immortalizing me in six

turgid lines of footnote.

A Kind of Knowledge

To seek it
to find it
to possess it
there are nine steps to be taken

reflection
recognition
identification
renunciation
incamination
transmission
initiation
personification
transfiguration

minute by minute
hour by hour
day by day
the path the road the way.

Maledicti In Plebe Sint

The pedants of deconstruction
are lathering each other's backs

with their own shit   who can
hate literature the most or con-

coct the most absurd algebras
of language   no birds may sing

in their trees   if there were
birds someone would shoot them

their books are written to be
read only as group masturbation

where has it gone the purity of
the young Hegel who hid the manu-

script of the *Phenomenology* un-
der his coat when Napoleon en-

tered Jena sic pallescet lux.

He Dreamed His Death

last night   it was neither an-
ticipated nor anything spectacu-

lar   no accident or illness of
which he was aware   no pain no

fright   it was no more than a
candle blowing out in a slight

breeze   he couldn't tell you
now how he knew what had hap-

pened but it was quite clear
to him that in an instant a

transition had taken place and
some voice inside him had said

(tho without any audible sound)
this is it   this is what you

had to be waiting for   he felt
no different than before but

he knew for certain that he no
longer existed in the same way

(or the same place) as before.

Digging Down To China

When we were boys (I was
four and my brother was

six) someone told us that
China was on the opposite

side of the world & that
you could get there by

digging   we wanted to see
the great wall and men

with pigtails and women
with bound-up feet who

couldn't walk   we took gar-
den trowels and dug & dug

& dug for days but we nev-
er saw the things we want-

ed to see   I guess I'm still
digging (there are mountains

of dirt all around me) and
I won't make it to China.

A Shard of History

Could it be that I am the one
who is the false Dmitri the

unknown whose nocturnal crimes
have terrified the city of Nov-

gorod   what do I do when I am
sleeping   am I a murderous

sleepwalker who remembers no-
thing the next day   is it only

my imagination that passersby
turn their heads and hurry past

me   are they whispering about
me in the cafés   although I

have no proof of what I fear
no blood on my hands or cloth-

ing should I give myself up
to the police   probably they

would only laugh at me   they
would take me for a madman

seeking notoriety   they would
put me for a few days in the

asylum for observation then
let me go   I would be free to

prowl again if that is what
I do   no if I am indeed the

false Dmitri my crimes de-
serve the final punishment.

Hic Jacet

civis pulvis et nihil
was all the inscription

that Cardinal Portecarrero
permitted on his tomb in

the cathedral at Toledo he
would not even allow his

name to be inscribed on it
just a flat stone with no

barrier around it so that
everyone would walk on him

a realistic man and though
he didn't know it a good

Buddhist here lie ashes
dust and nothingness R I P.

Index of Titles and First Lines

Biographical Note

Born October 30, 1914, in Pittsburgh, James Laughlin began publishing poetry, and short stories while in his teens, and as a twenty-two-year-old sophomore at Harvard University, he founded New Directions in 1936. Over the past fifty years, he has served as publisher to Ezra Pound, H.D., William Carlos Williams, Henry Miller, Kenneth Rexroth, Denise Levertov, Gary Snyder, and many others. As a champion of literature in translation, New Directions has published Boris Pasternak, Vladimir Nabokov, Pablo Neruda, Octavio Paz, and other writers from all over the world.

Laughlin's *Selected Poems* was published by City Lights Books in 1986, and Copper Canyon Press published new poems, *The Owl of Minerva,* in 1987. He has been awarded honorary degrees from Colgate University, Hamilton College, Duquesne University, Cornell (Iowa), Yale University, and Brown University. He has received the American Academy and Institute Award for Distinguished Service to the Arts, the Annual P.E.N. Publisher Citation, the National Arts Club Medal of Honor for Literature, and in 1988 was awarded the Prix Jean Malrieu for the French translation of his poems.

Laughlin presently divides his time between his home in Connecticut and the New Directions offices in New York City.

The type in this book is Fournier.
Composition is by The Typeworks, in Vancouver.
Book design by Tree Swenson
Book manufactured by McNaughton & Gunn.